Born in Stockport in 1955, 'Fitch' became a singer from the age of four. He travelled much of Europe and the Middle East working as he went. Living a hedonistic lifestyle full of women, drugs and rock'n'roll, adventures have filled his life all along, until a near fatal stroke in 2007 slowed him down a little. He attained a degree in Art History with Creative Writing with the O.U. and moved to Mexico to write it all down, and drink cheap tequila. *Re-Hab Is for Quitters* is his first book of autobiographical short stories; he is currently working on a three-volume autobiography, entitled *Shit Creek Survivor*.

I would like to dedicate my book to Graham 'Atty' Attwood and my mam and dad, the best people I ever met, wish you could have been here to see this.

Ian 'Fitch' Fitchett

RE-HAB IS FOR QUITTERS

AUSTIN MACAULEY PUBLISHERS™
LONDON • CAMBRIDGE • NEW YORK • SHARJAH

Copyright © Ian 'Fitch' Fitchett 2022

The right of Ian 'Fitch' Fitchett to be identified as author of this work has been asserted by the author in accordance with sections 77 and 78 of the Copyright, Designs and Patents Act 1988.

All rights reserved. No part of this publication may be reproduced, stored in a retrieval system, or transmitted in any form or by any means, electronic, mechanical, photocopying, recording, or otherwise, without the prior permission of the publishers.

Any person who commits any unauthorised act in relation to this publication may be liable to criminal prosecution and civil claims for damages.

All of the events in this memoir are true to the best of author's memory. The views expressed in this memoir are solely those of the author.

A CIP catalogue record for this title is available from the British Library.

ISBN 9781398462137 (Paperback)
ISBN 9781398462144 (ePub e-book)

www.austinmacauley.com

First Published 2022
Austin Macauley Publishers Ltd®
1 Canada Square
Canary Wharf
London
E14 5AA

Big thanks to Lilybeth Corte and Chris Boydell, for showing me the definition of true friendship. Also, to Mrs. Robinson, Head Mistress at Hollywood Primary School, for setting me on course for an amazing life of adventure and learning.

Table of Contents

Copenhagen 1985	11
Re-Hab Is for Quitters	16
Playa Del Carmen: A History of My Tattoos Episode One	29
Eilat, Israel, 5th November 1978. Part 1	32
A Very Special New Year	39
Playa Del Carmen: A History of My Tattoos Episode Two	48
Venice in Winter 'La Serenissima'	51
Up the Market Brew	53
Playa Del Carmen: A History of My Tattoos Episode Three	55
Eilat, Israel, 5th November 1978. Part 2	58
Mother and Sons	62
Eulogy for Laurence	67
Returning	69

Our Forgotten Humanity 75

A Beautiful Moment 78

Copenhagen 1985

My first stroke of luck was meeting a Danish guy called René Petersen when I was working the summer of 1985 on the Greek island of Corfu. René happened to be a brilliant guitarist who played in one of the top bands in Copenhagen. We'd get together and play in the campsite bar in the evenings; we hit it off straight away and quickly became good friends. He invited me to Copenhagen to stay with him and told me that he knew some people who could help me find a band. I had nothing else planned to do with my life and I was certainly in no rush to go home. So, I saved what money I could over the next few months and it was with a rucksack more full of excitement than clothes that I hopped on a plane into the future.

I arrived in Copenhagen at 10.30 am on a sunny mid-September morning in 1985, wearing my flip-flops, I immediately slipped and fell down the aircraft stairs. This I blamed on the Polish airline for supplying me with free vodka all the way. I managed to make my way to the main railway station, a huge cavernous building packed with people and luggage; this was where René had arranged to meet me.

'Fitch,' I heard my name, I turned and there he stood, tall and lean with his long blond hair tucked behind his ears, covered from head to toe in raggedy blue denim. 'Hey man,' I could tell straight away he'd had a smoke, 'welcome to Denmark my friend, you'll need this,' he said, holding out a metal bottle opener. My eyes lit up…what a thoughtful, genuine way to be greeted, especially for someone of the bacchanalian persuasion as myself. We shook hands and hugged, I was so happy. I still have that bottle opener on my key ring to this day.

René and Tina, his partner, took me in; they made me feel like part of the family. Their home was a bottom floor two-bedroom apartment in a suburb called Glostrup, a few kilometres to the west of Copenhagen. They had an old Alsatian dog called Miele (pronounced mee-ler), who took to me straight away…she was lovely and used to come into the bedroom and curl up around my feet, it saved having to fill a hot water bottle.

I couldn't afford to waste any time so I started to make money by going down to Strøget busking each day, using an acoustic guitar borrowed from René. René had taught me how to jump the trains so even the journey into Copenhagen was exciting every day, it may not be right but I'm proud of the fact that in almost two years I never got caught once. I used to play for half an hour at lunchtime and about the same in the early evening, this gave me plenty to live on, plus I made good use of my new bottle opener.

I loved this time of my life; it certainly improved my guitar playing, learning new tunes each day and having time to try out my own. The Danish girls were exceptionally friendly and so beautiful. In the last few years I've had three major operations on my neck and I'm sure the damage was done while craning it walking the streets of Copenhagen all those years ago. I remember I used to arrive at René's just in time for breakfast, most mornings from a different direction. It was a great way to learn the geography of Copenhagen. I looked upon it as getting my own back for the Viking raids on England years before, without the pillaging.

Then one Sunday morning in mid-October 1985, dear Lady Luck truly shone on me. I was aware that there was something big happening around the town hall square on that day because I'd sat and watched them building a massive double stage the day before, but when René spoke after breakfast, it blew me away.

'Fitch, I've had a word with the guy who's running the show and he said if you can get down there early enough, he'll let you play, just ask for Chris Friis.' So, with my stomach churning and my thoughts racing, I grabbed René's guitar and ran to the station, jumped the train into Copenhagen and went into the nearest bar for a beer. It was an unusually warm sunny day for October, ideal for an open-air concert. I kept going through what songs I should play, concentrating on the rockier ones where people could join in, best to play things they knew rather than try out my own, I thought.

I walked a couple of hundred yards to the backstage entrance. The clock tower chimed noon, it reminded me of how Gary Cooper must have felt at that time. There was a huge guy standing there, surrounded by people asking him all kinds of questions and I heard the name Chris being mentioned so I walked over. He looked down at me, then the guitar, and said, 'Hi.'

I nodded and replied, 'I'm Fitch, René Petersen sent me down; he said you might let me play.' He gave me the beady eye for a few seconds, then said, 'Okay, go get yourself a drink backstage and I'll give you a shout.' He gestured with his Schwarzenegger sized arm to a marquee behind the stage.

I lifted the tent flap to one side and stuck my head in, there were rows of empty tables and at the bottom end a makeshift bar. The first thing I needed was a beer. I checked the contents of my pockets; I could just about scrape enough.

'Can I have a beer, please?' I asked. The beautiful, mature blonde lady behind the bar looked at me and smiled the most perfect smile I had ever seen. I was at once hooked.

'Carlsberg or Tuborg?' she asked. I couldn't open my mouth, our eyes locked together for just a moment but it was enough…I was gone.

'Tuborg please.' She passed over the bottle and I lamely proffered some change.

'That's okay, it's free for artists,' she spoke the sweetest words I'd ever heard. We started to chat so easily it was as if we already knew each other. Her name was Lørna Østergaarde and she was apparently a world-famous hairdresser to the stars and was doing the backstage bar as a favour for Chris.

Suddenly, I felt an unnerving presence behind me and a deep voice uttered the words, 'Can you do half an hour now, Fitch?'

I got my guitar out and followed Chris up the stairs to the stage. The walk to the mike stand seemed to take ages. The vast empty space that greeted me was made to seem more so by a couple of dozen people gathered far below me. I launched into my first tune thinking, *well, I'm going to enjoy this even if there's nobody here.* My half-hour flew by and I walked off to the sound of silence, whilst basking in a feeling of elation. I packed my guitar away and headed for the exit.

'Where are you going?' It was Chris Friis calling me back. 'Stick around; I'll put you on again later.' I didn't need to be begged, so I headed back into the bar and the beautiful Lørna.

The tent gradually filled up with various types, I kept my head down and enjoyed the free beer. It was almost three o'clock when the unnerving presence appeared again; uttering those same words 'Can you do half an hour now, Fitch?' Rather unsteadily, I picked up my guitar and made my way to the stage. What happened next is permanently etched upon the inside of my skull…all I could see far into the distance were people. At once I thought, *it's a good job I've had a drink!*

What passed in that amazing half-hour took me up several levels. I remember people singing along with me, especially on the last tune, a reggae version of, *Knocking on Heavens Door*. I'd found my natural high. I held my guitar aloft and waving, I left the stage, leaving behind the cries for 'more'. I found the nearest thing to sit down on, within seconds Chris Friis was by my side handing me his business card and saying, 'Come and see me tomorrow, we'll sort something out.' Chris Friis was as good as his word and later that week I teamed up with three Russian guys and a Dane, a really talented band. I also found myself a beautiful lady to share it all with and she looked after my hair.

Re-Hab Is for Quitters

Through a milky haze, I could make out a giant hand coming towards me, WOW. It reached in and spread my eyelid open; a bright light hurt my eye.

'He's off his bloody head,' I heard a voice saying, 'we had better turn his morphine down a bit nurse, he's enjoying himself too much.'

Now this statement, coming from a doctor who had been called to my hospital bed in the middle of the night, sums up my attitude towards the subject of drugs. I've enjoyed certain of them for years. Some I totally despise. I don't care what anyone says there's nowt wrong with a 'toke', I've never heard of anybody killin' anyone when they've been stoned on weed, they couldn't be arsed. I remember a track by, *Cheech and Chong*, on one of their stoner albums from the seventies where a platoon of GIs in Vietnam was sent to destroy a marijuana patch and on the radio when asked by their captain how the men were doing the platoon sergeant replied, 'The whole platoon's wiped-out, Sir.'

I was in hospital about fourteen years ago; I'd had a stroke two days after an operation to remove a disc from my neck. I was told I'd been lucky to be in the hospital at the time or the chances were I wouldn't have survived. They were forced to rush me down to the theatre and cut my neck open to take out the blood clots that had chosen to have a party at the top of my spine. They explained to me before putting me under that I might not wake up and that if I did, I probably wouldn't be able to walk again. Well, I did wake up and immediately burst into laughter overjoyed that I was still here but when I tried to move my legs…nothing happened. My first thought was, *I'm sick of working anyway, early retirement for me then*, and that made me laugh even harder.

On a beautiful late spring afternoon in 1968; my mate Houghy and I were sitting underneath the middle tree of the three-towering horse chestnuts at the bottom of the school playing field, with the grunts from a game of rugby being played behind us in our ears. Marple Hall Grammar was a place where neither of us felt we belonged; all our mates had gone to the secondary modern but we ended up here amongst all the 'toffee-nosed gits'. Lunch break was over.

'Fancy pissing off for the afternoon?' Houghy said.

'Why not? The sun's out,' I replied, not giving a shit.

'We can have this,' he said, pulling a long, thin reefer out of his blazer pocket. My eyes widened, I'd seen and smelt one before but never had the chance to smoke it.

'Nice one. Where'd you get it?' I asked.

'Nicked it out of our kid's pocket last night,' he said, grinning.

'He'll fuckin' kill ya,' I said laughing, 'come on, let's get out of here this place does me fuckin' head in.'

We got up, jumped over the fence and headed down the path leading across to the woods. I looked behind me and

Houghy had stopped to light the spliff, I felt intensely excited and couldn't wait for my turn. I'd heard so much about getting stoned and now I was going to experience what it was all about. It hadn't been all that long since Jagger and Richards had been done for it and we'd just been through what the papers called, *The Summer of Love*, at last, I'd be a part of it and it felt right.

We came across a tree that had been felled by lightning, we sat on it and Houghy passed me the magic. I was only thirteen but from that day on I started to see the world differently. I became so aware of my surroundings and how beautiful it all was and how lucky I was to be alive and enveloped by it all. I felt as if I could finally hear the songbirds singing and understand the words; feel the breeze caressing me as it gently fluttered through the trees, the scent of the woodland flowers widening my nostrils and letting me know summer was almost here. All my senses came alive that day, I could pick out every individual instrument in the orchestra, digest the beat of life, and I wanted to sing. That's when I found my voice and realised what I wanted to do with it.

We also did a great amount of laughing, so much so my chest and lungs became so painful that I was in agony and snot hung down from my nose, becoming entangled in the embryonic bum fluff on my chin. I don't know how long we messed about down the woods but it seemed like minutes were lasting for hours; I remember I kept looking at my watch and I swear the hands never moved. When I finally walked in the back door at home I headed straight for the fridge.

'Where've you been? Your tea will be ready in a bit, you'll spoil your appetite.' I've no idea how many times I heard my mother say that, that summer.

As a kid, I had always been in a rush to grow up, I just wanted to get out there and travel. When I was very little, my granddad used to sneak me into the pub. I thought it was a magical place full of grown-ups using words I'd never heard before. He'd hide me under the table and pass me down a gill of mild. That's where I got my craving for the booze, I loved the smell and taste. I'm sure boozing was in my blood from the start, my great grandad was the landlord of the Conservative Club in Stockport for nearly forty years. I could change a barrel of beer by the time I was eleven and worked behind the bar in our local at fifteen. After failing to get into the RAF (I was deaf in one ear) I managed to get into catering college full time. If I have ever done one sensible thing in my life it was taking my granddad's advice to get a trade behind me, it meant I was able to get a job anywhere the wind blew me. As for dope I was not one of those that craved it, I enjoyed smoking it now and again and still do. I never got into it so much that it took over.

College was a great adventure and I absolutely loved it. No uniform and we were treated like adults, plus we could go to the pub at lunch times. I got expelled at the end of my first year for being a bad influence, although I had passed every exam they threw at me. My dad took me down there to plead my case with the head of the catering department, Miss Bown, and they took me back.

'You better start bloody behaving yourself, my lad.' These wise words from my father were totally ignored, of course. College made a big mistake by putting me in a group that were far crazier than the one I'd just been kicked out of. This was the summer of 1972, I'd already started singing the 'blues' with some great musicians, John Mayall's brother Rod was one, and I had discovered the wonders of an array of chemicals. I did try to do the right thing once, after I left college, I went into Hotel Management for two or three years. This was just to keep my mother off my back really, anything to keep the peace. It ended when I walked out of a top job and went 'walkabout'. Eventually, in the red-hot summer of 1976, I landed in Newquay, Cornwall. Through my old college friend Tom, I got a job as a waiter at The Bay Hotel on Fistral Beach. It was one long party and also, not long after I arrived, the scene of my first interaction with those lovely men in blue uniforms.

I awoke to the sound of my door being kicked in; I turned over and stared up into the face of a grinning uniformed policeman.

'Wakey, wakey…rise and shine!' Very original, I thought.

'Would you mind keeping the noise down please,' I said calmly, glancing at my clock, 'it's six in the morning and a Sunday.' At that moment, my eyes caught sight of a plain-clothed copper standing behind my door. I watched as his hand moved to lift up the cellophane cover of a freshly cleaned jacket that was still on a coat hanger hung on the back of it. I saw him put his fist inside one of the pockets and pull out a nice big chunk of hash!

'You bastard,' I hissed at him, quickly sitting up, 'you fuckin' bastard!' The plain-clothed guy then took an evidence bag out of his pocket and put the lump in it. I knew he had planted it for two reasons, a) the jacket had just come back from the cleaners and hadn't been worn, and b) we had only been smoking cannabis oil for the past few weeks, we couldn't get hold of any hash. There was a big argument going on in Billy's room next door; they must be bustin' him too.

'Come on Ian, get up and get dressed,' the uniform said, at least they knew my name, which was nice.

I got up and put on a t-shirt and shorts. The uniform then grabbed my arms, forcing them around my back and put the cuffs on. The other copper then emptied the ashtray into a plastic bag, went through my drawer and even took the bottom sheet off my bed! 'Good luck with that,' I thought, with the action that had seen lately, you could stack it against the fuckin' wall never mind get it out of the door!

Then it came, 'Ian Fitchett I am arresting you on suspicion of the possession of...' blah blah blah.

They led me out of the door along the corridor past the other staff rooms; Billy was still arguing and giving his coppers a load of grief. There was a 'Black Maria' waiting downstairs and I was unceremoniously shoved in the back. About ten minutes later, Billy followed headfirst.

'Fuckin' bastards,' he shouted out.

'Did the fuckers plant it on you too?' I asked him. He nodded. Billy had only got back from visiting Bolton the day before and we had spent most of the Saturday night going around town selling everything that he had brought back, which was speed and trips. So obviously somebody must have had a big gob and the cops had got wind of what we were up to.

We were taken to the main cop shop in the centre of town; there we were locked up for a few hours than formerly charged. They released us about two that afternoon with a notice to appear in the magistrate's court the following Thursday. So, we headed for the pub.

'I'm gonna fight it,' Billy said, 'bastards are not getting away with that trick with me.'

'They were after us, man,' I said, 'there's no way you'll win Billy, they'll be on your back till you get out of town.'

He was adamant he was going to go for it and get himself a solicitor. A couple of days later, the owner of the hotel, Mr Hicks, passed by me. He asked what I was going to do and I told him I was just going to accept it and take what comes. He agreed with me that it was best, I could forget about it then and they would leave me alone. He was okay with me; he could have sacked me if he wanted to.

I've never been proud of just accepting what happened but it turned out okay, I got fined £90, which I agreed to pay at £5 a week. Billy ended up going to Crown Court in Truro where he was fined £150 and had to pay all the costs! I was ordered to attend but was never called as a witness. They left me alone and I stayed for a couple of years and had a ball. I still go down there at least once a year to stay with an old mate of mine, Pete. I've had no time for the men in blue ever since though, bastards!

I've always dabbled in things that I shouldn't, it makes life exciting, I absolutely hate boredom. The problem is, I have a very addictive personality and if I like something, that's it. This applies to the full range of playthings available to me, my music, booze, drugs, and women.

Take women, for example. I've always tried to be myself, no airs and graces, warts and all, so when you meet someone you really like, things should be straightforward, yes? They see you as you really are and both of you are getting on together as well as a team of arsonists. Then why, usually after about the first three months, do things start to change? Or put another way, why are you expected to change? What you are is the reason why they fell for you in the first place! I can understand in some cases that you could be happy to go along with it because you are so besotted that you don't care and are willing to settle for what you have and then spend the rest of your days trying to please her and keep her happy. That's why the majority of my relationships have lasted on average about four months, although there have been a couple of exceptions where pure lust has taken control of my genitals and I've become a total jellified idiot.

One morning in the early spring of 1986, whilst looking after a friend's apartment in Copenhagen (where I was living by this time), I received a phone call from England; it was my second wife, whom I had married the previous November at Copenhagen Town Hall. She asked me if I was free to come home for the weekend as it was her mother's sixtieth birthday and there was going to be a big party at her house in Wales. The band had nothing on so I said I could make it and we arranged to meet at our place in Macclesfield on the Friday teatime and then drive down there.

When I arrived at the flat there was no sign of her, I thought that she must be just running late or something like that but when it got to eight o'clock I became a bit concerned. So, I phoned her mother's house in Wales, that's when I got a shock. Her mother hadn't a clue what I was on about, she didn't know anything about a party and it certainly wasn't her birthday! What the hell was going on? I tried a few of her friends and they hadn't seen her and had no idea where she was, so I thought, *Fuck it, I'll go over to Stockport and see some of my mates.*

After a very enjoyable weekend and after still trying to contact my wife without success, I flew back to Copenhagen on the Monday morning. Going straight to the studio to see the guys I was greeted with a chorus of, 'Where the hell have you been?'

'What do you mean?' I said in amazement. 'I've been back home, I told you I was going.'

'Your wife's been here all weekend, she came to see you.'

'WHAT?' I shouted.

It turned out that our planes must have crossed in the air. I later found out that she had been messing about with my manager <u>and</u> a friend of mine! She'd done this because she couldn't control me anymore, I think; she was rich and thought she had bought me. It had only been three years since I'd discovered my first wife had been having a fling with my brother! I was still fucked up from this and should never have married this one. This news totally destroyed me. That was it, I didn't give a fuck anymore, and I couldn't work with the band again, so I called my 'friend' in Christiania.

I'd tried 'smack' before and it hadn't done much, only made me throw up and pass out but this time I was determined to go where it wanted to take me. I wanted to forget everything, to take the pain away and turn my brain into mush. The only lights I wanted to see at the end of the tunnel were the flames from the crematorium. I soon got into the knack of using a needle and gained the ability to control the throwing up until the urge to do so melted away altogether. I entered a dream world where nothing mattered, least of all me. Cleanliness and eating went out the window. The only occasions that time meant something were when I needed more and had to see my 'friend'. I finally closed the door on everything and everyone, completely unaware of approaching extinction and free-falling headfirst into an abyss of dead souls.

I used up my welcome from people that I knew quite early on, people soon turn their backs on you if you have a death wish. It scares the shit out of them when they're faced with their own mortality; they were only protecting themselves. I was spending more and more time hanging about in Christiania, dossing wherever I could with whoever would let me stay. I sold almost everything I possessed and learnt how to steal. Weeks turned into months and I became adept at living on the streets and finding places to crash and new people to use. It would take something terrible to shake me out of this nightmare.

That is something I've never spoken about before and find it difficult to recall now thirty-odd years later. I awoke one morning after a heavy night in a darkened room lying on a strange bed, not having a clue as to where I was. I could sense there was someone else crashing out at the bottom of the bed but thought nothing about it. I found the bathroom and splashed water over my face, dried myself off on a filthy towel and started to look for my jacket. Back in the bedroom, I could see that the guy on the bed had crashed out on it so I shook him, nothing. I couldn't wake him so I grabbed my jacket and tried to pull it from under him. That's when I felt his arm, it was icy cold. I looked at his face; his lips were blue and his eyes half-open and lifeless. Fuck! He was dead!

I felt the urge to run and get out of there. I wrenched my jacket from under him and crept out into what was the lounge. It was dark but I could make out various bodies fast asleep on the floor and furniture. I slowly edged my way towards what I hoped was the front door praying no one would wake and that I didn't step on anyone. Successfully reaching it, I lightly turned the door handle, it opened outwards and I slithered through onto what appeared to be a landing. Gently closing it behind me, I ran down the stairs and finally out into the street. Sweat was streaming from every pore and I couldn't breathe.

'What the fuck am I doing?' I asked myself. I was terrified; I knew I had to get home. But how?

There was only one thing I could do. Ring my father and plead for a ticket home. Here I was, a thirty-one-year-old total fuck up running back home, a failure. That's how I felt. I went around to see an old girlfriend, Lorna, to ask if I could use her telephone. Lorna was a well-known hairdresser who I had met not long after arriving in Copenhagen and we'd spent about six months having an affair; it ended when it became too dangerous. Her man was one of the biggest gangsters in Denmark. When she opened the door and saw the state I was in, she hugged me and wouldn't let go. Luckily, he was abroad.

I broke down and poured my heart out. Then this beautiful, beautiful lady picked up the telephone and bought me a ticket to Manchester that was leaving the very next morning. It's impossible to describe how I feel about this woman, to this day, I still cry when I think of Lorna.

In 1991 and again in 1994, I hit rock bottom through the usual mix of a broken heart, guilt, living on five E's a day, and attempting to drink the world dry. In both those cases, I ended up in the fruit farm or using the correct term, the psychiatric ward.

I've tried for years to describe what happens inside your head during a breakdown, it's the most difficult, heart-searching topic imaginable. The closest I've come to diagnosing the symptoms is the term, *total sensory overload*. It's where you feel every possible feeling but all at the same time, shame and hurt, pity and hatred, love and volatility. You can't speak because you're scared of upsetting anybody, the telephone rings but you can't answer it. If there's a knock on the door, you hide behind the sofa and shake. You live in darkness keeping the curtains closed because the daylight hurts your eyes. If you look up at the sky, all you see is the inside of your eyeballs, blackness. You never leave the house. The list is endless; full of totally unexplainable things that you can't help but let happen. This goes on for weeks.

Then one day you find yourself in a sanctuary, a place of quiet. You're surrounded by people but they leave you alone. You lie on your bed saying nothing to anyone, refusing visitors even though you know they are hurting too.

Gradually, very slowly your days start to get a little brighter; you're able to chat with fellow sufferers. You have your first laugh, that's the breakthrough, that first laugh. You start to retrace your steps, finding your way down the various branches to the main trunk that is your path in life. You figure out where it all started to go wrong, it's not easy, it's very painful. The hurt makes you shed buckets of tears, each tear bringing more relief.

Then you have an urge to get out of there, to try again, you want to give it another go. You've learnt the things to avoid, recognise situations before they happen. On the outside, you cope with the way people avoid you. They cross the road when they see <u>you.</u> They don't realise that <u>you</u> are grateful for this, those people are not your friends, which saves you having to tell them to 'fuck off!' You have become strong again, maybe even stronger. It just takes time.

Well, that's about it. I'm in my mid-sixties now, survived two strokes, and have just finished a degree in Art History and Creative Writing with the Open University. I gave up women some twenty years ago; I realised I wasn't cut out for all that relationship business, very messy. Now my life is peaceful, in fact, I would go so far as to say that having that last stroke saved my life! Crazy, yes. Now I'm off to sip my Tequila and where did I put that spliff?

Playa Del Carmen: A History of My Tattoos
Episode One

I discovered Playa del Carmen over twenty years ago. The people that I worked for back in England owed me lots of holidays so I made a deal with them, they buy me two weeks in Mexico plus spending money, and we call it quits. They got me two weeks at somewhere called, *Club Bananas*. It was situated at, what was then the northern end of Fifth Avenue. Some of it is still there, closed up and in ruins by the look of it.

I spent almost every day of the two weeks walking back and forth down Fifth Avenue, escaping the regimentation of 'all inclusive', which looked nothing at all similar to the one you see before you today it was just a well-worn dirt track, sparsely populated by any buildings. I ventured into one of these for a drink on my way back from the village to the complex one late afternoon. The place was empty except for a young shaven-headed guy behind the bar, against which he was leaning reading a book. I found a stool and sat down.

I asked if he had any Mezcal, something I had heard about and was curious to try. His eyes widened in a look of what seemed to show disbelief. He asked if I was sure, I nodded. With a shrug of the shoulders, he went out the back and returned with a large brown label-less bottle. He then proceeded to pour some piss-coloured liquid into a shot glass. Smiling broadly, he pushed it towards me.

Over the next hour or so, the length of time is truthfully a blur, I began to realise why he was smiling when he gave it to me. I had another one just to make sure it was working. The walk back that day was an interesting event. The birds were very, very noisy, I remember, and I'm sure the sun had got closer because everything was ten times brighter. The dirt track had taken over the guise of a fluffy marshmallow…it was absolutely marvellous.

Needless to say, this became a part of my daily routine, and I vaguely remember one evening, on my way to the 'Blue Parrot', where I was allowed to get up and sing with the band that was performing that night, a version of, *Honky Tonk Woman*, I think it was. The bar turned out to be the now world-famous, *Tequila Barrel*, no less, in its infancy. The 'guy' behind the bar, whose name was José, is still one of my closest friends to this day. In fact, just a few months ago, on the morning of my mum's funeral, I received a video call from Sweden and it was José and his son, calling me from his home there. It was such a beautiful gift on such an emotional day by such a very special person.

You might be wondering what this has got to do with tattoos. Well, about eight or nine years ago, on one of my frequent visits, I had the logo for the bar inscribed in ink on my left upper arm. This was duly photographed and the picture was affixed to one of the tables in the bar. No point looking for it nowadays, it disappeared when the old place was demolished a couple of years ago and replaced by the new one. I would love to find that table and claim it for my place here in Playa…which I am hoping to make my permanent home now, amongst some very special people.

Eilat, Israel, 5th November 1978. Part 1

The day started out as normal; we got up and did our usual jobs, me scrubbing the decks and Linda tidying up. We were not taking the boat out today, so apart from Tepper and Yuda calling round to check on things, we could take things easy. The only decent music we had on board was, *Year of the Cat,* by Al Stewart, so that was belting out through the deck speakers. To this day, I can still remember every word of that album. A couple of berths up, Tim and Duncan were getting ready to take out a load of Club 18–30 idiots for the day. This was great because that meant there would be plenty to drink tonight. You see, they always brought more booze than they needed, which Tim and Dunc found many hiding places for. It was also their turn to cook dinner, so a party was on.

Linda and I had come a long way since we left home in May, having got the Magic Bus from London to Athens. The first night in Athens, we had our tent robbed whilst we were asleep! Luckily, they did not get much, just a bit of Greek money. We then got a boat to Crete where, the first day we were there, we got jobs on a campsite just outside of Hersonissos called Caravan Camping.

We spent the summer there, having a great time and meeting many beautiful people. Then we decided we wanted to go to Israel for the winter. We managed to save up enough to get the boat to Rhodes, where we could catch a ship to Haifa via Limassol, Cyprus. When we got to Rhodes, we found that we had just missed the boat by one day, the next one being in another six days. Not having much money, we thought it would be wise to get out of town and find somewhere quiet to make camp for a few days, so we got the bus to Lindos.

It turned out to be a smart move because we were able to put our tent up in a field just behind the beach. We managed to survive by clearing the sand of empty bottles and taking them back to the bar at the end of the beach. For this, we were fed and watered free. Also camping in the field with us were a couple from what was then Rhodesia. It was great to sit with them in the evening's drinking and listening to what it was like out there, hearing it all first-hand instead of just the news back home. Some of it was shocking. Anyway, after five days, we had to get back into town to catch the ship. It was a ship an' all. They took us out to it in a little dingy, it was still dark and the sea was throwing us all over the place. We had to climb up the side of the ship and with our rucksacks on it was no mean feat. Eventually, we found somewhere on the deck to lay out our sleeping bags and get our breath back. I had a look around and came across a large sofa just inside one of the lounges. This became our sleeping quarters for the whole voyage.

Two days later, we arrived in Haifa, having stopped off in Limassol for just a couple of hours. We counted our money. It totalled £11 between us. It was now the beginning of September. We got the bus to Jerusalem and luckily found a

Kibbutz that let us stay for free for a couple of nights. What a place Jerusalem is, no wonder so many people have tried to conquer it. You feel as though you are at the centre of the world. It was beautiful, stunning. I almost turned religious. Almost!

After a couple of days of doing the sightseeing trip, we had to get to where we could find some work. So, we caught a bus to Eilat. We had heard that that was where the hotels and the tourist attractions were and sure enough, it was true. Within two hours of arriving, we had been offered three different jobs at three different hotels! We found a bar, where we sat and spent the last of our money, and made up our minds which to take. We picked one called, *The Bell Hotel*, the main reasons being that it was next to the marina and the living in accommodation was okay. I worked as a chef and Linda as a chambermaid. The head chef Jean, a Belgian guy, was a right character. He would come into the kitchen in the morning, tell me what to do, and then bugger off to the bar down the road and sit and get drunk all day! It was great for me; I was left to my own devices all day and you can guarantee Linda and I ate really well. We lived like kings for a couple of weeks and apart from a bit of trouble we had with an Arab guy who would not leave Linda alone, it was great.

During those first couple of weeks, we had got to know quite a few people in and around the marina and we had spread it around that we were looking for work on the boats. Sure enough, we were offered the jobs that we were doing at the time of this story. I did the cooking, deckhand work and Linda was serving and looking after the housekeeping. The boat was called, *The Vagabond D' Azure*; she was 30 metres in length and had two massive General Motors engines. She was beautiful. Pure luxury. The captain was a lovely guy called Tepper, a big man with a full beard and the engineer, a crazy bloke by the name of Yuda. They both lived somewhere in Eilat, and we only saw them maybe four times a week. We got on fantastic with both of them. We could not have lived better if we had been millionaires.

So back to that fateful day. Linda and I spent the afternoon lazing about on the top deck, drinking cheap plonk, and smoking even cheaper grass. The origins of the grass were bizarre. I was working away in the kitchen of the hotel one day when this Canadian guy turned up at the back door asking for a job. Anyway, cutting it short, he ended up KP'ing and moving into the room next to us. He knocked on our door one night and asked if I could give him a hand. I went with him into his room and he showed me a black bin liner full to the top with grass! He said, 'Please, take some of this off my hands, will you?' That was the hand he needed! I always like to help a fellow traveller; it's the rules of the road, so I filled two carrier bags up. Then he told me the story behind it. He had spent the last few months living with some Bedouins out in the desert and they had given him this as a gift when he left! We were still smoking the stuff nearly eight weeks later, and we had not even half-emptied one bag. That 'we' includes Tim and Duncan, who thought all the stories about the Promised Land were true after all!

It was about 4.30 when we heard the lad's boat coming into the marina. There was also a Canadian girl working onboard with them but for the life of me, I cannot remember her name. There is no one I can ask either, having lost touch with everyone involved. Therefore, apologies to whomever you are out there, that is, if this ever gets read. Anyway, the guys had big smiles on their faces, a good sign. When they had tied up and unloaded all the idiots, Dunc shouted across to say to give them an hour or so then come over. About six, we joined the crew, not only was there wine and beer in abundance but lots of leftover food as well. Life could not get any better, booze, free grass, food, and great company.

It was a beautiful sunset, the sea glowing bright red with the reflection off the mountains. Now, I know why it is called the Red Sea. I do not know who it was but someone happened to remember that it was Bonfire Night. It was so easy to lose track of what day it was, the way we were living. I certainly remember whose idea it was to take the speedboat out for a run. Mine! I have had some crazy ideas in my time but this one is up there near the top. Anyway, I clambered over to our boat and managed to get on board the Dory (a type of speedboat with the steering wheel set towards the back). I got the motor running and cast off. I steered myself around to pick up the others. Surprisingly, they all managed to drop down on board without falling in and we set off.

It was now dark and the moon had not yet risen above the mountaintops. I slowly steered us out of the marina and as soon as we were through, I opened up the engine and we headed off down the Red Sea into open water. It is hard to describe the euphoria, and the togetherness we all felt as we hurtled, at full speed into the darkness, it really was magical. We had been going for about ten minutes when the engine started to struggle, making a loud whining noise. I turned off the motor. Leaning over the back and pulling the outboard up towards me, it did not take a genius to see that we were entangled in some fishing nets. Because of our inebriated state, none of us could stop laughing. It did not take long to get us free and we carried on, leaving a foaming-white wake behind us. Then it happened.

All of a sudden, the sky lit up. We could hear a loud voice but could not see where it was coming from. It sounded mechanical. Without thinking, I swung the wheel to my left and did a complete U-turn. Opening up the throttle, we flew off back to where we had come from. I glanced behind me and all I could see was a bright light trying to pick us up in the water. Adrenalin took over, I cannot remember anything anybody was saying and I just aimed at the entrance to the marina. After what seemed like ages, we eventually passed through the harbour entrance. I pulled up by the Vagabond; I remember telling someone to take the wheel, while I jumped on board with the mooring rope. I tied up and told everyone to jump out and disappear back to their boat. Linda and I shot below and dived into bed.

Well, all hell broke loose. The noise from above sounded like a platoon of stormtroopers had just burst into a Parisian Café. I shot out of our cabin and flew through the galley up the stairs onto the deck. There facing me, pointing machine guns at my chest were about five or six Israeli soldiers. All I could think about was their boots tramping all over my spotlessly scrubbed deck, 'Get them fucking boots off my deck!' That is all I managed to shout before I was kicked to the floor and pinned down. Linda was pulled screaming from the galley. The next thing, we were dragged down the gangplank and thrown into the back of an army truck. Tim, Dunc and the Canadian girl soon followed. Half a dozen soldiers jumped in, picked us up, and sat us down with one of them sitting in-between each of us. The truck then took off at some speed.

We all looked at one and another as if to say, 'What the fuck was that?' I remember looking at Duncan and almost bursting out laughing but thought better of it. I asked Linda if she was all right, she just shrugged her shoulders but I could see her eyes were filling up. I gave her a wink and a smile and mouthed some words that I hoped would help. After about fifteen minutes, the truck screeched to a halt. The tailgate dropped down and we were each grabbed by a soldier and dragged off the back of the wagon. We were shoved through a metal doorway into a large, white, square-shaped room. It had a desk in one corner and behind it there sat the biggest, hardest looking bastard I had ever seen. Some words were exchanged in Hebrew, so none of us had a clue what was going on. Tim, Dunc, and I were then dragged through a door, which led down a short corridor into a large open space; there were more doors with barred windows in them. I tried looking to see what was happening to the girls and I could see that they were following behind. Next, we were pushed towards a door that had been opened by the big hard looking bastard and thrown in. The door clanged shut behind us.

A Very Special New Year

I think it's fair to say the 'Assassins' were shitting themselves. I'd been under contract to the Hell's Angels for the last few months and been well taken care of, anything I've asked for I've got and I mean anything. In fact, I was buzzin'. I'd heard all sorts of things about their place and all good, especially for a dedicated hedonist like me. 'We've never played anything like this before', Brett said sounding a bit nervous, 'what are these guys like, man?'

'They ain't never done me no harm,' I said, putting on my best redneck accent, 'they've been looking after me reeealll gooood.' I don't think this eased his nerves so I passed him a spliff. Brett's the bass player with 'The Assassins', a Heavy Metal band from Birmingham; they'd been over here in Copenhagen doing a few gigs with my band over the festive season. Brett is so small he disappeared when he strapped his guitar on. It was so funny to see him on stage with two feet sticking out of the bottom of his huge Fender bass and his head hidden behind a pair of huge milk bottle bottom glasses, just like a Spike Milligan drawing. But what a great guy, in fact, all five of them are. I'd been having a ball with them and their hilarious accents since they've been over, dossing on their hotel room floor most nights. My band was pissed off because they've hardly seen me except on stage; I could tell when we went to pick the gear up this afternoon they were a bit frosty, never mind, they'll get over it. It's not often I got the chance to get wasted with a load of crazy Brummies'.

Brett and I were sitting up front of an old converted ambulance which the band drove over in; the other guys were all in the back with the gear. After every pothole, we could hear them bouncing around, dropping bottles and cursing their hangovers. It didn't stop me and Brett from enjoying the spliff though.

We were on our way to their last gig; playing for the Hell's Angels at their headquarters out in a place appropriately called Tune. We were in the process of trying to find it through the huge Christmas trees growing on either side of the track. It's hidden away somewhere in the middle of this forest a few miles outside of the city. My band members wouldn't do it but as these guys were relying on us for the PA, I've had to come along to do the sound. Thank god for a clear sky and an almost full moon beginning to blossom above the treeline lighting up the way. It had been dark since lunchtime and it's about seven now. You were lucky if you got an hour's daylight over here in the winter. That's why there are so many suicides; depression sets in you see, it's the busiest time of the year for the drug stalls in Christiania.

We turned a bend in the track and Brett slammed the brakes on. 'What the fuck!' he hissed through pursed lips, dropping the spliff. Without thinking, I dived to the floor to find it. The sound of bottles dropping and loud cursing came from out of the back of the van.

'What the fuck you doing up there?' someone kindly asked.

'Brett dropped a bleedin' spliff,' I replied, equally as pleasant.

'Oh, okay,' came back a very understanding Brummies' voice.

'Have a look at this Fitch…' whispered Brett. Having retrieved the joint, I slowly raised my head above the dashboard. There in front of us was 'Fort Apache'. We were in the middle of a John Ford movie.

'Jeez…keep an eye out for Indians mate, John Wayne's on his way with the fifth Cavalry.' I whispered back. This was surreal, either that or it was the best hash I'd ever had. A full-scale old western fort stood silhouetted against the moonlight; I could even make out a couple of guards with rifles patrolling the parapet above the huge double-doored entrance. Brett slowly inched the van forward towards the doors; I wound my window down and stuck my head out. A faceless voice shouted down from the parapet, 'Who are you?'

'Chris Friis sent us, we're the band,' I shouted back.

There was a time-lapse that seemed to go on forever then the same voice shouted, 'Wait there.' So, we did. A nervous hush fell within the van and if anyone spoke it was barely in a whisper. After about ten minutes we could hear movement and the sound of heavy bolts being pulled back. We'd changed movies now we were in a Hammer Horror, wondering if Igor was on duty. One side of the door opened slightly and a colossal hairy leather and a denim-clad figure stepped out, looked the van up and down then strode towards my open window. He was carrying a shotgun. Just at that very moment, someone in the back chose to let go of an excruciatingly loud fart. This was followed by a muffled schoolboy giggling.

'I am happy that you leave that outside,' said the colossal Hell's Angel in broken English. I tried to keep a straight face but failed when Brett burst out into hysterical laughter. I'm sure the big guy almost smiled.

'You cannot unload at the moment we are having a meeting. Bring the truck and follow me.' He turned back towards the doors; another guy stepped out pushing them wide open, I noticed he wore a pistol on his belt. Brett, having calmed down a bit, drove as instructed and we passed through into a large square with brightly lit wooden buildings all-round the compound. There were lines upon lines of amazing motorbikes parked up, I could make out they were mostly Harleys; they looked so beautiful gleaming in the moonlight. We could hear raised voices coming from what seemed to be a long hall on the far side of us. Our guide signalled for us to stop by the door of a two-storied building, Brett and I got out and went round to open up the back, the lads spilt out as did the stink.

'Which one of you dirty fuckers did that?' I said pretending to rub my burning eyes.

'I did,' said the drummer, 'and proud of it too.' We were led up a steep staircase to a room on the first floor. There was the audible sound of deep breaths being taken as we entered. There were three enormous fish tanks running along the whole length of three of the walls. They were full of massive piranhas!

'Wow,' we all said in unison, 'what the fuck!'

The big guy spoke, 'Wait here, I will be back.' He really said that, honest. We settled onto two large brown leather sofas in front of a roaring wood burner, with the light from the fish tanks it looked pretty cosy. Within two minutes he arrived back carrying two crates of Tuborg Gold plonking them down on the floor between us. 'Have that for now, they are finishing to make the stage.' he said and left. I flipped the top off a beer with my lighter and lit a fag, the others did the same.

'This is okay ain't it?' I said, laying back on the big comfy leather sofa.

'You seen the size of them fuckin' fish-man, wonder what they feed 'em on?' said Brett fascinated.

'You're about the right size for 'em Brett,' said Nick, one of the guitarists, 'better watch out.'

'Piss off!' he replied. Just then a small black cat jumped up onto my lap and made itself at home, this indicating an unexpected gentler side to the Hell's Angels I thought unless it was actual fish food. I noticed there were a few running around. I shivered.

Over an hour later, I grabbed the last bottle from the second crate. 'Hope he brings some more,' I said, 'I've got a hell of a thirst coming on.' By now it was half-past eight and I was beginning to wonder what was going on, after all, we had to unload the van and get the gear set up and sound checked. We heard footsteps coming up the stairs and two different colossal guys came in.

'We've come to help unload the truck guys, follow us.' They spoke with Geordie accents…marvellous it gets better and better. We were taken across the square to the building where we heard the raised voices earlier. Brett brought the van over only just missing a line of bikes, images of them dropping like dominoes entered my head. He shouldn't be allowed to drive with those eyes, jeez! We entered through a large door into what was a big dormitory full of wooden bunk beds and passed through this into an enormous hall. Along the opposite wall, there was a long fully stocked bar with Hell's Angels sitting on stools the full length of it, others were sitting at tables or stood in groups. To our left, a couple of them were finishing off hammering the last nails on the stage. Before we knew it, the Geordie guys had started bringing in the gear from the van, all I had to do was tell them where to put it. I found a table and placed it a good distance from the stage and started setting up the mixing desk. A Hell's Angel, the smallest one I'd seen, came up to me and introduced himself, 'Hi I'm Stefan, I'm in charge if there's anything that you need just give me a shout.'

'Hi, I'm Fitch, we could do with a couple of extension leads if you've got 'em,' I said, 'and where can we plug in?' He showed me the electric points, then disappeared for a minute and came back with the leads. 'Thanks a lot,' I told him, 'I could do something to keep me awake?' I cheekily asked.

'Come with me,' he said. We walked over to the bar and he said a few words to a guy who sat on a stool who promptly took a tissue from a holder on the bar, then tore one corner off and placed it flat in front of him. He then reached into an inside pocket and pulled out a plastic bag absolutely brim-full of pink speed, there must have been ounces in it. Using a small spoon, he proceeded to heap spoonfuls of the pink powder into the centre of the piece of tissue. When there was what looked like two or three grams of the stuff there, he looked up at me as if to say, 'is that enough?' I nodded and he folded the corners in, twisting them together and made a little dolly bag out of it and handed it to me. Wow, I thought, *that'll do us all.* I was just about to turn and walk away when he touched my arm and gestured for me to swallow it…whole! He looked at me and smiled, I thought, *what the hell?* And popped it into my mouth and swallowed, he looked at the barman and nodded, the barman brought me a beer. I took a slug and washed it down thinking, *shit, I'll be up for a fuckin' week with all that!'*

'Everything okay now, Fitch?' It was Stefan. I said, 'Magic man, thank you again.' He smiled and said, 'If you and the band need more beer, I've put a few crates by the stage, help yourselves.' I thanked him for the third time and went back to my desk. Not long after, Brett came over.

'What was all that about?' he asked. I told him what had just happened. 'Can you sort me out?'

'Go over there and ask him ya self,' I told him. 'Don't be scared, it's cool.' He trundled over on his little legs, after five minutes he came back with a big beam on his face.

'Don't tell the guys', he said, 'they'll go mad. They don't like me doin' it when we're playin.' I nodded and shouted towards the stage, 'You lot ready to sound check yet?'

'Give us a few more minutes,' Brett said, almost skipping back towards the stage.

Nick shouted from the stage a few minutes later, 'Ready to go Fitch.' This was the first time I'd done all of this on my own. We usually had our own sound guy but I'd been involved with it so many times I was confident enough, especially now my head was beginning to take off. Whoosh…there it goes! It seemed to all go smoothly; all they really wanted was to be as loud as possible so I just turned everything up to 'eleven'. That'll blow the roof off!

'Sounds good,' it was Stefan, 'can you go on about twelve-thirty, after the food and the fireworks?'

'Sure, whenever you want. How long do you want them to play?' I asked him.

'Up to you, a couple of hours, okay?'

'No worries,' I told him, 'I know the bass player and me could play all night.' He laughed and walked off.

I was beginning to really like these guys, there must have been a few hundred of them here from all around the world. I've seen colours here from as far away as Brazil but by far the rowdiest are the British groups, bloody typical, the others seem to be staying away from them. The same as I've always done on my travels.

I couldn't help but notice that the number of scantily clad women had increased in the room. The traffic between the bar and dormitory had begun to flow freely, I wondered if that was on the house too. These guys certainly knew how to throw a party! I checked my watch, only ten minutes to go. The crowd was starting to head outside through a double door at the back. I looked for Brett and spied him at the bar talking to death to one of the Geordies, I couldn't see the other four guys. I caught Brett's eye and pointed to the door and started out that way. Outside opened up into a lawned open space surrounded by forest. In the middle, revolving over a fiery pit skewered on the biggest spit ever was a full-sized steer!

'I wish I was hungry.' Brett said next to me.

'A bit over facing though, don't ya think? I couldn't eat a full one.' I replied. I noticed that his eyeballs were hanging out on stalks; he'd have a job hiding those from the band. Speed takes away your appetite so there was no chance we would be having any, though I found out where the others were, in the queue plates in hand.

At midnight a humongous loud bang went off somewhere nearby and everybody cheered and hugged each other, Brett and I included. Neither of us was ready for what happened next. Explosions and bright colours were flying upwards from every direction; did we jump, we were at the centre of the best firework show you could ever imagine and my brain was doing exactly the same inside my head. I never believed I would ever hear hundreds of hard as nails Hell's Angels in a field going 'ooh…haa' like big kids. The scantily clad ladies came hurrying out, wrapped in blankets and began jumping up and down, shrieking right in front of us, bare breasts bouncing before our very large eyes. 'Think we'll remember this New Year for a while,' I whispered in Brett's ear. He looked up at me and his eyes, enlarged by the milk bottle bottoms, matched the moon for brilliance. We both fell into uncontrollable hysterics…that lasted for the next two days!

Playa Del Carmen: A History of My Tattoos
Episode Two

One of the main reasons why I fell in love with Playa is the number of smiles you see everywhere. Makes a huge difference from the misery surrounding me in Manchester (why I left it so many times), even the rain here is in a hurry to get back up to the blue, it quickly steams and soon evaporates. Whereas, where I come from it likes to hang around, turning down the corners of your mouth, sometimes for days!

'La Rana' is a totally different kettle of fish than the Tequila Barrel. This is a really unique hacienda style establishment. I came across it a good few years ago now, just by following the 'crowd'. By crowd, I mean mostly the people who live and work here in Playa del Carmen, mostly from other parts of Mexico and various countries around the world. Having been a nomadic seasonal worker for a large part of my life, I have never thought of myself as being a tourist. I have usually found myself easily blown down the same pathway to find and get along with people of 'the same ilk' as it were. Like-minded people like this tend to be amongst the most interesting and fun-filled people around, happy to share life's ups and downs because they can recognise you and feel your heart. I have been so, so lucky to meet and call my friends, many beautiful hearts here in Playa. My upper left arm is now also adorned with the logo of 'La Rana'.

I simply could not resist having a large green frog, standing cross-legged, holding a cocktail and smoking a cigarette, embellishing my skin. A frog acting like a lounge lizard, perfecto! I have seen only one other, worn by a gentleman who is from New York, I believe. We were introduced once by the owners Thed and Pia, not long after I had had it done. Another determiner is written in chalk on a blackboard on the wall outside, 'If you don't drink, how will your friends know you love them at 2am in the morning!' Again, perfecto!

Getting to know the people here has made it impossible for me not to feel at home. In fact, I feel happier here than I ever did at any time in Manchester. Like I have achieved something by finally finding where I belong. It has taken me many years but as the old adage says, 'You have to kiss a lot of frogs before you find the right one.' I might have altered that a little but you know what I mean or you will if you keep following my writing, either that or insanity lies ahead! Anyway, 'La Rana' is my frog…hahaha. I love nothing more of an afternoon than sitting, arms leaning on the railing overlooking Calle 10, watching the world go by. Just smiling, drifting off with my imagination, going where it wants to take me. The biggest decision being, 'shall I have another Modelo?' This might sound a bit crazy but having my last stroke I am certain saved my life. It succeeded in doing something that no living person has ever been able to do, slow me down and many have tried. So nice to finally chill…and how lucky was I to find the 'perfecto' place to do it.

Venice in Winter 'La Serenissima'

La Serenissima, the most serene one, as Venice is known. The most beautiful city in the world. It's true that once you have been there, you will always want to go back. You seem to leave a small piece of your heart behind every time you visit, that's true in my case.

I remember the last time I was there; it was purely by accident. I'd had an invitation to go to Rimini to stay with an Italian lady who lived there, I'd met her a few months before in Mexico, but Rimini airport closes in the winter and with-it being January, the nearest airport was Venice. The plan was to fly to Marco Polo and then get the train to Bologna, then on to Rimini. So, I managed to organise some free time and figured out that it would take me a day and a half to get to Rimini.

Well, I got to Venice station and gazed out over the Grand Canal. I couldn't believe my eyes. I was mesmerised. How magical Venice looked. Covered in a fine layer of snow with the lights glistening off the water, so sharp and clear. I'd never seen anything so fairy-tale in my life. After getting my breath back, I quite easily found myself a cheap room for the night, the joy of going at this time of year, and I went out for a stroll around. I have to say that that evening was one of the greatest highlights of my life. So much so, I ended up staying another night! Gone were all the memories of hot, sweaty, mosquito-bitten nights down narrow alleyways. Don't get me wrong, Venice is magnificent any time of the year but it becomes something extremely impressive, wondrous even, in the dead of winter. I will never, ever, forget the sight of Saint Mark's Square in the early hours, with the glow of a full moon shining off the fresh snow. Absolutely stunning. I think, as you may imagine, Rimini was a bit of a let-down after that, in more ways than one.

I managed to do the same thing on the way back, staying at the exact same hotel, in the exact same room. I even managed to catch the same view of Saint Mark's Square, not quite a full moon this time though and the snow had turned to slush. I honestly can't recommend 'La Serenissima' enough. I was there by myself but I can imagine what it would be like with someone you truly loved. Maybe if I had arranged to meet my little Italian friend in Venice instead of Rimini, things might just have turned out somewhat differently. Ciao!

Up the Market Brew

How do you describe melancholia? The dictionary states thus, *a mental condition marked by persistent depression and ill-founded fears.* Well, that about sums it up! It's exactly how I felt as I approached the steep brew up to the old marketplace. It had been many years since I had been out like this; well past midnight, soaking wet, missed the last bus home and totally broke.

The idea was to take a shortcut home through the old marketplace, the very theatre where I had spent so many past years creating my own history in one shape or form, from the bands I sang with to the food I cooked, all distant memories now flooding back.

From my right, I could detect a familiar aroma. The Fish Shop. The same smell hanging there as it had been doing for hundreds of years, just as my granddad would have sampled on his way to the Pack Horse on Saturday lunchtime to play Don with his mates. I wondered how the lady, Mary, who worked there was getting on. I remembered that time I went to Dublin, one of the first pubs I went into in Temple Bar I heard a voice shout out "FITCH!", I turned around and there was Mary, in the middle of a crowd of inebriated Irishmen.

Needless to say, it would have been rude not to join them, having gone all that way.

The rain dripped down the collar of my soaking wet jacket, which by now was as heavy as a cobbler's last. Shortness of breath made me reach for my inhaler. Thank God for chemicals! I'm sure this hill was never this upright. The bright lights and heavy thud of the live music were willing me onwards and upwards.

Finally, I reached the summit. There, outside the Bakers Vaults, were no Sherpa's but man mountains dressed in black, huddled under, *Stella Artois,* golf umbrellas. The full moon, at that very moment, found a gap in the clouds and then, for a split second, I knew how Jake and Elwood Blues felt the last time they went to church. After a few seconds of getting my breath back, I took a long disbelieving look around the empty market square. Flippin 'eck! What a change. At last, someone from the Town Hall had finally got off their backside and done something. The place was spotless. There I was, surrounded by freshly painted history. I always knew it could be like this. What a pity that someone couldn't have done it years ago when there were still lots of people around! Ah well! Only another four miles to my lovely warm bed!

Playa Del Carmen: A History of My Tattoos
Episode Three

I absolutely love the sun. Coming from near Manchester it's mandatory because it is seen so rarely that they teach you about it in schools! I have chased the big yellow giant for years, working and living under it wherever I could. I must be a cold-blooded being, I only get going when I warm up. A bit like the little gecko that lives with me at the moment. We have an arrangement; I don't tread on him and he keeps the insects down, it works well.

It was natural for me to drift towards Zenzi; the sounds blew me that way. It's on the beach and has a bar, vital ingredients. But more important is the music it provides. I have been a singer of songs since I was four years old, in and out of bands all my life. Making music runs through my veins. So, imagine how I felt the first time I asked the band playing there if 'I could do one?' Memo, whose band it was, said, 'Okay.'

I was nervous, not about getting up to sing. I've never been nervous about that but about my neck. This would be the first time since my stroke that I had sung, I had only just learnt to walk again and needed a stick! The operation I had to have meant that they were forced to open me up from the base of my skull to the bottom of my neck, about 8–9 inches I think (I've never seen it!), shaving the bone so thin so as to get at the blood clots having a party in my spinal cord! It meant that I didn't know whether my neck would snap or not because for those who haven't seen me in action, I tend to jump around and scream quite a lot. That was I don't know how many years ago, and I have been 'doin' one there ever since. Sometimes they let me do more than one! 'Fitch, can you do another?' Is a cry I have heard or was that a dream? You'll have to get down there sometime to let me know.

The other night I was making my way down there to sing and my false teeth became loose. Searching through my pockets, I discovered that I had neglected to pick up my 'tooth glue' off the table. Panic struck! Visions of my plates landing on some customer's plates whilst they were enjoying the marvellous food came into my head. I burst out laughing in the middle of Fifth Avenue. So, I had to make a detour to find a pharmacy.

Currently, I am making music with some of the best guys I have ever had the pleasure to have played alongside. Sadly, Memo went up to play at the great gig in the sky a few months ago. I hope I have been able to show my gratitude to him and all the others for the privilege of being allowed to 'do one'. As with my other tattoos, it felt good to get the Zenzi logo inked onto my skin, this time my upper right arm (the left being a bit overcrowded). I haven't had any of my tattoos done to be a showpiece, they are for me personally, to always remind me of how lucky I have been/am to have found my paradise, my slice of heaven. I hope that I will never take up too much space on this beautiful planet of ours, my tattoos hopefully though, will continue to take up all the space they can find on my skin.

Eilat, Israel, 5th November 1978. Part 2

I opened my eyes and there, not six inches away from the end of my nose, was the biggest cockroach I had ever seen. I just stared as the beast ambled by on its trek up the wall. It must have already scaled the equivalent of Everest to get this high, I was perched on a top bunk! Turning away from Sherpa Kafka, leaving it to metamorphose on its way, I rolled over. There opposite lay three sets of metal-framed bunk beds end to end along the length of the facing wall. I looked straight across from me at two faces I recognised, Tim's and Duncan's and after a quick glance around the room, at nine Arab ones I didn't.

The three of us looked at each other and simultaneously burst into hysterical laughter. This was what can only be described as one of those 'bloody 'ell THAT was some night out!' moments. We had woken up in an 'elegantly decorated' Israeli prison cell. We heard a commotion outside the cell door and then from the small gap under it appeared several blue plastic plates with what was apparently our breakfast or lunch, none of us were aware of the time, having had our watches taken from us on check-in. As the plates kept coming, the Arabs dived in and scuffles broke out between them, I was consciously making a mental note of the hierarchy amongst my fellow inmates, in particular one giant of a man. The three of us calmly sat back and watched until it had died down and they had all got theirs, then we picked up the final three that were left. It was a good job that we weren't hungry. A tomato, three slices of cucumber and some chopped lettuce accompanied by a stale bread roll. The door opened and a dirty-looking Arab guy wearing what was left of an old string vest brought in a tray of mugs half-filled with some sort of grey steaming liquid, after the same rush we again grabbed the remaining three.

'Room service could be better,' Duncan said. The three of us burst out laughing again, by this time we were getting some strange looks from our Arab friends. I suppose sharing a cell with three crazy Brits was as much a novelty for them as it was for us being locked up with nine Arabs.

The toilet facilities consisted of a hole in the floor tucked away in an alcove a few feet distant from the end of my bunk. Things that I witnessed there were too disgusting to mention, luckily all the time we were in there I only ever needed to pee, proving that mind over matter can work, I just refused to go. We sorted out a sleeping rota too, making sure that one of us was awake at any one time. The goings-on during the night was eye-opening the least, sometimes not even at night. I've seen many mind-blowing things in my life but nothing compares to what went on in that cell, thankfully I was not alone and I still have nightmares about what would have happened to me without the presence of Tim and Duncan, two great guys that I will always carry in my heart.

On the second morning, we began to worry. No one had been near, no consulate official, no police or army…nothing, not even our employers. The only outside contact was when the 'string vest' came in with the grey liquid at mealtimes. When we did try to find out what was going on, from any guard we saw from the cell door window, all we got back was 'no understand' and shrugged shoulders of indifference. I was able to contact Linda by shouting through the door; she was in a cell around the corner with the Canadian girl. She seemed to be coping okay; there was nothing I could do anyway. All we could do was sit and wait and play I-Spy.

'I spy with my little eye something beginning with SDC' was one of my best ones, it went on for hours.

'Do you give up?' They both nodded, 'Squat down, Crapper!' I ducked the flip-flop that came my way.

On the third day, we started to get really worried, I could tell; the laughter had stopped. There had not been any sign of anything happening. Surely someone knew we were in here. The morning of the fourth day, the door opened and a very well-dressed policeman entered the cell flanked by two of the guards. His eyes opened wide when he saw Tim and Duncan.

'What the hell are you boys doing in here?' he said surprised at the sight of them. Tim and Duncan explained what had happened to us. The police officer shouted some words in Hebrew at the two guards; it was easy to see he wasn't happy. 'Leave it to me,' he said and left the cell, the door closing quickly behind him.

'That was bleedin' lucky,' said Tim, 'that was the Chief of Police, he's been out on our boat a few times, he's sortin' it.' And sort it he did. Within an hour we had been taken from our cells and allowed to get washed up, we were then driven to the local courthouse. The outcome wasn't too bad either, for the other four, that is, they all got fined the equivalent of a fiver and I got the equivalent of twelve months' probation! They had something like twenty charges against me.

One of the lads had been allowed to nip out to a bank and draw enough money to pay the fines; we were set free and made our way back to the marina. There we found a strange woman on the boat who handed us an envelope containing all the money we were owed, she also told us to quickly pack all our things and get off the boat…we had, of course, been sacked. This we did, then said a tearful goodbye to everyone over a beer at the local bar. The other guys had managed to keep their jobs by blaming me, which was fair enough. It was still only early afternoon and we managed to catch a bus up to Tel Aviv.

There was no way it would be prudent to hang around, not with twelve months' probation hanging over my head. Our wages, because we hadn't been paid since we took the job, were enough for us to catch a plane to London the next day. The worst bit was having to hitchhike up to Manchester mid-November in only a tee-shirt, shorts and flip-flops, bloody freezing. We got to Linda's house and her father was so glad to see her and have her back safely that he gave me a lift home to my mam and dad's and he thanked me for looking after her, if he only knew.

I obviously didn't learn my lesson because the following summer I was locked up in Corfu! I'll tell you about that one later…

Mother and Sons

I moved back home after mam and dad's car crash in April 2005, catching the bus up the next day. The phone call the previous night had said, 'There's no need to worry, they're alright.' I could tell by my brother's delayed response he was lying. Leaving Newquay was a ball ache having only just got settled; I'd been there about eight weeks and had got my old job back at the Bay Hotel, after a break of almost thirty years and I was due to get the Head Waiter's job.

The bus journey was a tortuous nine hours through driving rain all the way, made even worse by my mind ripping like a tornado through all the various scenarios; how badly were they hurt? Am I an orphan? I arrived at the hospital absolutely piss wet through at about six-thirty that evening, after first calling at a nearby pub for a couple of large Remy Martins. Eventually, tracking down my father's ward, I found my brother and his tribe gathered around the bedside. It was a shock to see dad; his face was a bloody mess, having had his false teeth smashed, they had proceeded to cut his mouth to pieces. His right hand was heavily bandaged, and his thumb stuck out at a crazy angle. Both his knees were buggered up too. My eyes filled up, poor sod. For the first time I realised how old he had become, he had always seemed the same age to me and it wasn't eighty-two.

He was conscious and his eyes lit up when recognition set in, he attempted to smile. I held his hand, the good one that is, and tried hard not to burst out laughing at the sight of him, this being my usual reaction in times of great upset. He could see this and tried to shrug and laugh himself. That's something we have always had in common; I think it was passed down through my dad's experiences in the Second Parachute Brigade during WW2. He did a lot of shrugging then I suppose, trying to understand the whys of it all.

'What've ya been doing, you daft bugger?' I said, squeezing his hand. He just looked up at the ceiling and smiled, revealing his mutilated gums. My brother signalled for me to walk outside with him. I nodded, pressed my dad's hand once more and followed.

'Where's me mam?' I asked.

She's in intensive care,' our kid replied, 'they don't know if she'll make it. All her ribs are broken and they've punctured her lungs, plus she keeps having heart attacks.' My stomach went cold and my heart started pounding, shit, shit, shit! Everything seemed surreal; this is what happens to other people or in a crap soap opera, not to us. As we made our way to the IC unit, the walls of the corridors seemed to close in, I felt my chest tightening and my breathing became difficult. I took my Ventolin inhaler from my jeans pocket and had a couple of deep draughts. My lungs began to relax. We continued down two or three more corridors and up a floor by lift. Neither of us spoke, this was usual as we never got on. It's funny how I always called him 'our kid', he's almost six years older than me. I'd found it hard to even look at him since he had had a fling with my first wife about twenty-five years earlier. I had only kept things sweet at family gatherings because of my mam and dad; I had no plans to ever see him again after they had passed away but I found myself praying that this wasn't the time. I would have to work that one out later.

On arrival at the IC unit, we were told that our mam had been moved to the High Dependency Unit down the corridor. There were only two beds in the ward; my mam was on the left surrounded by various machines bleeping away, all plumbed into her frail white body. She was wearing an oxygen mask tightly strapped to her face; I later found out that they had done this because she had kept tearing it off. Just like me mam that if she didn't like something, you soon knew about it. Apparently, she'd been giving the nurses hell, when she was awake that was.

A nurse approached us and after enquiring who we were, said, 'The doctor would like a word with you in the office, this way, please.' I looked at my brother as we followed the nurse out of the ward, he didn't return it. We entered a small room where a young Asian doctor sat at a desk nursing a computer.

'Come in,' he said standing up, 'please, sit down,' my brother sat in the chair offered and I leant against a cupboard opposite. 'I'm afraid I have some bad news about your mother,' it was a scene from a movie. 'Her condition is so serious that we feel it would be better not to attempt to revive her if she has another heart attack.' I could feel the anger and astonishment swelling up in me till, bang, the valve blew.

'So, you're just going to let her die?' I shouted. 'Don't you believe in fuckin' miracles?' The doctor seemed to go pale and shifted backwards slightly, startled by this.

'Calm down, Ian, they're doing their best,' our kid hissed.

Doing their best! They're gonna let her fuckin' die…' my head was going crazy. This wasn't happening…I needed a cigarette. I walked out of the room and headed down the corridor. The next thing I remember, I was outside the hospital attempting to turn a soggy fag paper into some semblance of a cigarette. It was still pissing down; I couldn't decide whether it was the rain on my face or tears of anger. The cigarette was having its effect and I began to slowly get my thoughts together. Crazy how something that kills you calms you down, I should go relaxed then. Did I really shout at that doctor? I put my foot on the fag end and slowly walked back to my mother's bedside.

When I got back, my brother was still sitting talking to the doctor in his office, ignoring them, I walked past and went to my mother's bedside. The nurse very kindly brought me an armchair. My mam's eyes were closed and she looked peaceful, probably because she was loaded on morphine. Something I was to enjoy the feeling of a couple of years later when I had a stroke! Marvellous stuff, I highly recommend it.

Sitting there watching over my mam brought back memories of all the rows we had had over the years, and there were plenty. Like the time she didn't speak to me for two years after I left my wife! It's a dilemma I have lived with all my life but I loved her. I always rushed back home when she was ill. My dad was a star; I know he only wanted a quiet life, understakable after his upbringing and war experiences.

'Feel better now?' It was the voice of my brother behind me, bringing me back in his sarcastic manner.

'What do you think?' I said.

'I'm off home now,' he said calmly, 'no point in hanging about here.' He started to walk towards the corridor. I couldn't help myself. I got up and went after him.

'You're going home…what the fuck's up with ya, man?' I almost screamed. I was boiling over again. 'What about me mam? Ya can't leave her like this.'

'I'm not staying here watching my mother die!' He turned, it was the first time he'd raised his voice or showed any emotion. 'Well, you can fuck off!' I whispered under my breath. 'I'm not leaving her to die on her own.' With that, I spun around and went back to my armchair, praying that my mam couldn't have heard any of that.

As it turned out, I sat in that armchair for almost a week holding mam's hand, only nipping home for a shower and a change of clothes when our kid turned up for a couple of hours. I kept going down to my dad's ward two or three times a day. He was causing trouble down there, saying he wanted to go home and he was going to sign himself out. After some stern words from both of us, he stayed put. It transpired that my belief in miracles was not misplaced and after a week, my mam was moved out to a normal ward where she continued to get better. I'm writing this a few years later, she's eighty-seven now and I'm still at home taking care of her, my dad died a couple of years ago, aged ninety.

Eulogy for Laurence

I first met Laurence when we both worked at the 'Market Porter' pub in Borough Market, London, I think in about 1996–7. Time's a bit of a blur these days. He worked behind the bar and I was the chef. I used to arrive for work at 8.45 every morning and there would always be a steaming hot mug of coffee waiting on the bar for me, put there by Laurence, without fail. Then we would have a chat for about 15 minutes before I started work. I used to look forward to those few minutes each day. I also remember going out for smoked salmon and cream cheese bagels at 5 in the morning whenever I had stayed at his apartment near Smithfield market, both of us having been up all night and being the worst for wear but laughing. Laughing is what I remember most about Laurence because that's all we did. We just clicked. One time he came to see me one afternoon when I worked as the head chef at 'The George' facing the Law Courts in the Temple. We got a couple of bottles of red wine and went to sit on a bench in the Temple gardens. We just sat there and drank the wine out of glasses we'd nicked from the pub, it started to rain quite heavily but did we move? Did we hell, as fast as we drank the glasses filled up with rainwater…special times with a special guy. I used to go up to the Lake District when he had the

'Howard Arms' in Brampton some weekends, even taking my parents on one occasion. He also came down to visit me and my parents near Manchester; they got on really well, which everybody did on meeting Laurence.

I was the one who was supposed to go first, after all, you sussed out that I had come out there to see you for what I thought, at that time, could be the last time because of the state of my health after having my second stroke. Compared to me, you were an Olympic athlete, a giant of a man...I never thought you would be the one to beat me to it, it was one race you could have let me win, bastard! At least now I know there will be a big mug of steaming hot coffee waiting for me on the bar when we team up again 'brother'. Till then, I will have to get used to you not being on Skype, I'm so sorry that I missed your last call mi amigo, it's something that I will regret forever, but I like to think that we knew each other well enough to know how it would have gone. Just in case, I'll keep your account open man...Until that joyous moment we meet up again, Laurence, I love you my brother...always, FITCH xxx.

This eulogy was written at the request of his wife and was read out at services for Laurence in both Johannesburg and Cape Town, South Africa.

Returning

Twenty-two years is a long time in anyone's book. That is how long it had been since I had last walked down Strøget, the main pedestrianised shopping street in central Copenhagen and, as any Dane will eagerly point out, the longest in the whole of Europe. I'd been reminded on the flight over about the mindset of the Danish male, having sat amongst ten Vikings, on their way back from working a six-month contract somewhere over Liverpool way. The embarrassment on the faces of the gorgeous Danish airhostesses was all too apparent, which helps to explain why a high percentage of Danish women marry foreigners. The redeeming quality of the flight was the Turkish person I sat next to, Iken, he was just as pissed off as the girls and he had been working with them the past six months!

Now, I cannot begin this tale without mentioning two things. First, the enormous part that drinking alcohol played in the proceedings. Denmark, being the Centre of the universe as far as beer production and consumption is concerned, has an attraction that is unavoidable for all dedicated Brahms and Liszt experts everywhere. I, being of the bacchanalian persuasion, find it to be heaven on earth. Having lived there for quite a while in the mid-eighties, I can vouch for its place in the grand scheme of things. Wake up to a beer, go to sleep with a beer. People stop for a beer on their way to work in the mornings! Highly civilised, I say.

However, that does have its downside. About seven years ago, I rang an old girlfriend of mine, who I hadn't spoken to since I'd left. When I asked her how she was, she replied, 'I'm fine, apart from just having had a liver transplant!' Secondly, the women. This is the wrong time to be stuck for words. I kind of knew what to expect when I first came to Copenhagen, having worked on a campsite on Corfu for a few years, you get to meet so many beautiful women from all over the world. But nothing prepared me for what happened in my head when I arrived in the capital of Denmark. In the last two years, I've had two major operations on my neck and I'm sure the damage was done in the first few weeks I lived in Copenhagen! Everywhere I looked, there was nothing but Miss Worlds. It was unbelievable. Just nipping out to the shop could take days. All you had to do was buy a girl a coffee, sit and chat for a while and they would take you home. So sweet. But, eventually, you get used to it and don't even notice. It's true!

As you might have guessed, I'm on a bit of a nostalgia trip. I was curious to see how life had turned out for some of the guys that I had been in the band with. I'd managed to track down André, the genius Russian keyboard player and main man on My Space. We'd sent a few messages to each other and he seemed glad to hear from me, giving me his phone number and telling me to ring when I got in town.

So here I was. Thirst things thirst, beer. I walked down to Kongens Nytorv, the square at the bottom of Strøget, to find this little underground bar that I used to frequent. It was still there. After a few, and several attempts to use the public phone outside, I asked the barman to call André for me. This he did and passed on a message, André said he would meet me at 6pm in the Hard Rock Café, next door to the Tivoli Gardens. *Rather appropriate,* I thought. Three hours to kill. Dangerous.

I began to stroll back up Strøget, calling in various hostelries along the way. Memories came flooding back. Passing all the places where I used to stand and busk, in all weathers, snapped strings flying everywhere. People's faces, long, long, forgotten, appeared just like yesterday. All the street people I got to know and love. It's amazing how when you find yourself in bad situations, something, or somebody always turns up to make you smile.

As 6pm approached, I felt myself getting a bit nervous. *At least he's alive*, I thought, last year I went back to Corfu to see the guy I spent years working for, only to find out he'd died five years before! Mind you, his wife put me up in her hotel, which was nice. Half pissed; I turned up at the front door of the Hard Rock Café. I found my way to the bar; it was at the furthest end from where I'd walked in and I had a good look around. No sign of a very tall Russian, just your usual pseudo that seems to frequent these types of places, they never listen to conversations but sit around staring, hoping to catch a glimpse of somebody famous and get noticed themselves. I ordered a pint with a Jack Daniels, ignoring the stares!

I would like to tell you a little bit more about André. A pure genius and a nice guy to go with it. I remember one time in particular; I had been in a pretty bad car crash. The car in question was being driven by our then manager, Chris Friis. He had asked me to drive his car back as he had to pick up a van from somewhere. On the way, he managed to park it under a giant articulated wagon that pulled out in front of us. I could see what was about to happen and luckily, I passed out. I came to in an operating theatre in a hospital somewhere in Copenhagen. Looking around me, I could see Chris on the next table having his trousers cut off. My head felt like an atomic bomb had exploded inside it. The crash had taken the roof clean off and a good piece of my head with it. To cut things short, after a few days in the hospital, in which André and Michael (the bass player, also Russian) came to see me each day, bringing me the necessities, André and his girlfriend Marina, looked after me at their apartment on Amager while I got stronger. This I am eternally grateful for. This was only one of many instances where his generosity came to the fore, without question and not a second thought. A truly generous human being.

Suddenly there he was. You couldn't miss him. At least a good six inches above anybody else inside the bar. I waved and he came over. After a strong handshake and a hug, we commenced to get lashed. We talked like twenty years had been twenty minutes. Amazing. The only difference being he had shaved off his moustache. His hair was still touching his arse. We were even drinking the same drink as each other, Jack Daniels, in place of the usual vodka of olden days (surely a sign of rock'n'roll maturity). For the first half-hour, it was like a non-stop question and answer session, finding out what had happened to various people, then André suggested that we get something to eat. So, we knocked back our drinks and left. We didn't go far. Just across the road from the Tivoli Gardens, there is an Irish pub called Mrs Magee's. We crossed the road and entered. A gorgeous blond (what else), showed us to a table. André ordered two large Jack 'n' Cokes. We ordered our food; he had a steak and I some Mexican dish. It was then I gave him the pressie I had brought for him. The complete collection of everything Jack Bruce had ever done, dating from the late 50's up to the present day. Proper educational stuff. André had been stuck in Russia up until 1984, so all this early British music would have been hard to get hold of. He seemed to appreciate it, so much so he shouted up two larger Jack 'n' Cokes. Now, when I'm drinking, I find it very difficult to find room for food, so while I just shovelled mine around the plate, I kept the supply of large Jack 'n' Cokes coming.

The conversation was magical and more so as the evening wore on. Finally, we asked for the bill. It came and André immediately picked it up and placed some notes in the folder, waving away my earnest attempts to give him some money. Next, André asked me where I was staying. Now, I had prepared a list of hotels within my price range but I hadn't done anything about booking one, just in case the evening ended up with me crashing at André's in a total heap. So now, I showed André the list and picked one that I knew was just down the road on Vesterbrogade. During two final large Jack 'n' Cokes, André telephoned the hotel and booked me a room and phoned for a taxi.

We made our way outside. The night air somehow seemed warmer than that in Manchester. Then, André handed me his mobile and said, 'speak to René'. Well, I was gobsmacked. René was the Danish guy that I met in Corfu, and the main reason I ended up in Copenhagen in the first place. It was something I wasn't expecting. Apparently, he lives a good distance away from the place now and has been having a hard time of it. We both, at least, had something in common, we'd both been in re-hab a couple of times! The taxi arrived and we both got in. The hotel was only five minutes away, André helped me to the door. I rang the bell, the door buzzed, I pushed and it opened. We looked at each other, automatically hugged, with my foot in the door keeping it open, André said, 'Ring me tomorrow.'

'Okay,' I said. He got back in the cab and drove away. I got the lift to the reception, picked up my key and found my room. Wasn't much, bog on the landing but very clean, heaven when you're full of Jack Daniels. I lay on the bed, looked at my watch, 'fuck it,' I'm going out! It's only 2am, and if anybody knows Copenhagen, Vesterbrogade is the Red-Light area of Copenhagen. So, I found my way downstairs, opened the door, and I was gone!

Our Forgotten Humanity

What has happened to the world? Think about it. I'm coming up to being sixty-six years old and I have never known it to be so bad to exist on this planet as it is now. Luckily, I just missed the Second World War but I was born into the aftermath of recovering from it. My father fought in the war from the age of eighteen to being almost twenty-four when he got de-mobbed. He was in the Second Brigade of the newly formed Parachute Regiment; he volunteered for it and did thirty-two jumps, he would have stayed in, he once told me but he had caught Malaria, from which he suffered on and off for the rest of his life (and he was ninety years old when he died).

I think about the world he fought for, to create for every one of us, and look at what it's like now. He fought so we could all be free from tyranny, to be able to live peacefully and be able to make our own choices of what to do with our lives. As I grew up, I would use this creed as an excuse for my behaviour, 'my dad fought the war so I could be free to do what I wanted.' What I wanted to do was just have a good time, sing, travel and party. And I have certainly done this to great excess as some of you reading this will be aware of. But

I always read and listened and watched and enjoyed gaining knowledge.

History was always my favourite subject, learning about the past was so interesting. I'm now so grateful that I did because somewhere along the way as I came down, I realised how important it is to learn from the past. I wish many more people would have done this. If there was ever a time that we needed to learn from the past, it is now. We need to look at what the world was like leading up to the Second World War, the events that happened the two decades before. The Spanish Flu that began just before the end of the First World War, the pandemic killed almost 100 million people and we have one now. It took years for that to end and so will this Coronavirus if we don't act differently and become less selfish in our attitudes. Thankfully, we have more education these days, a greater amount of medical knowledge than back then. What we have to do is listen to these people and believe them, not invent crazy conspiracy theories, these scientists are trying to do their jobs and destroy this disease. Same with the governments, it's the first time for them to deal with anything like this, we must not invent situations just so as we can go out and party with our friends. Nobody on earth wants this to continue, listen and work together. Back then, people had a lot less than we do now, life was hard enough without a pandemic, young and old looked after each other, and they had lost a whole generation of young men!

It is no wonder that people have lost trust in the 'dickheads' that run our various countries, but who's to blame…we are, we voted for them! The reason being our lives had become a lot better and we were having a good time, we stopped really caring about the world. We took our eyes off the ball. We stopped caring about other people, our own selfishness blinded us, we became the 'me, me, me' generation. This must change…and very soon, otherwise, there will be nothing left that is worth caring about. I could make a long list of the 'dickheads' but we all know who they are, we have to use our collective power and wise up, work together and flush them away. There are enough of us to do it! Together we can put them on the run, we are scarier than they are and they know that. Speak out, join up…let's get our humanity back. This is the time to do it, just look back at the history of what happened in the twenties and thirties….if that doesn't fill you with fear for your future, I'm giving up.

A Beautiful Moment

I had managed to get my mam out of that diabolical nursing home, where she had been for only five or six days and taken into hospital on the Monday. The doctors and nurses were doing everything possible to keep her alive. For four days my mam kept asking me to tell them to leave her alone and let her go in peace, she'd had enough and wanted to die. On the morning of the fourth day, I sat with the registrar and pleaded with him to let her go…he agreed it would be for the best and that they would make her as comfortable as possible and let nature take its course. This they did and later that afternoon she fell asleep. She stayed like that peacefully until just after 3pm on the Saturday afternoon when she suddenly sat upright, grabbed my hand and with her eyes still closed, she smiled and a huge tear fell from her right eye…I put my other arm around her shoulders and gently laid her back down on the pillow…that was it, it was all over…